A special thanks goes out to
Megan Marshall
&
Addison Marshall

Thank you for your
Contributions to this
New series.

This book is dedicated to my Aunt Mary and to all those who wish to make an incredible memory.

When I was very young and new to Salt Lake City, my father would drop my brother and I off at our aunt's home to spend the weekend on occasion. The dichotomy between the life I experienced at home and under her roof was astounding. At our small apartment, we always had what we needed but never frivolous playthings that children often gravitate towards. But at her place, there were VHS players with an entire collection of Disney movies, A freezer full of popsicles, Chests full of toys to entertain ourselves for hours, board games that she played with us well into the night, a Nintendo, a large yard with a dog and name brand cereal!!! It was an oasis of intoxicating stimuli that never ceased. All these wonderful objects were a joy to behold but pales in comparison to my most precious memory of my aunt Mary and her home. Just before bed, she would make sure we had brushed our teeth, then off to a room filled with gadgets, gizmos, and a comfortable bed. She would tuck me in, turn on a very soft night light, then proceeded to brandish a book. Unfortunately, I cannot remember which one it was or what the subject matter conveyed. As she began to read, I experienced an indescribable feeling of security, warmth and wonder that penetrated my being. The emotions emanating from this experience etched a permanent memory upon my consciousness. I struggle to find a series of words that would do that moment justice, but that moment is the very reason I decided to write this book. I want every child to have an opportunity to capture their own precious memory. The bond and memories created when a loved one reads to a child just before they slip into a state of dreaming can be wondrous. These series of books are made to be read by loved ones to children to create a permanent precious moment. Enjoy!!

Goodnight Africa.

When the sun slings low,

All of the savannas critters are in for a show.

As daylight fades,

The stars glisten in a spectacular way.

Let us visit this unique vale,

Along with the many creatures,

Who have spent a long day on the trail.

Goodnight Lion,

May your dreams confide strength as you reign,

Far from the troubles of maintaining your mighty mane.

Goodnight Hippo,

May your dreams gift you good luck,

If you could ever get out of this muck.

Goodnight Giraffe,

May your dreams imbue you with glee,

Once you're untangled from this wretched tree.

Goodnight Crocodile,

May your dreams grant you peace as you drift underneath,

After these silly birds finish cleaning your teeth.

Goodnight Elephant,

May your dreams bestow upon you delight,

Once you have shut out the ruckus of night.

Goodnight Warthog,

May your dreams allow your imagination to swell,

After you come to terms with your smell.

Goodnight Hyena,

May your dreams allow you to reminisce as you submit,

If only you could silence your giggling fit.

Goodnight Kudu,

May your dreams grant you an evening stressless,

Once you've unwound your horns from this mess.

Goodnight Baboon,

May your dreams elevate your conscious state,

When you recover from all the marula you ate.

Goodnight Heron,

May your dreams allow you to soar to incredible heights,

If only you could keep yourself from squawking tonight.

Goodnight to all critters,
Both large and small.

Goodnight to this mighty land,
That houses them all.

Goodnight Africa!

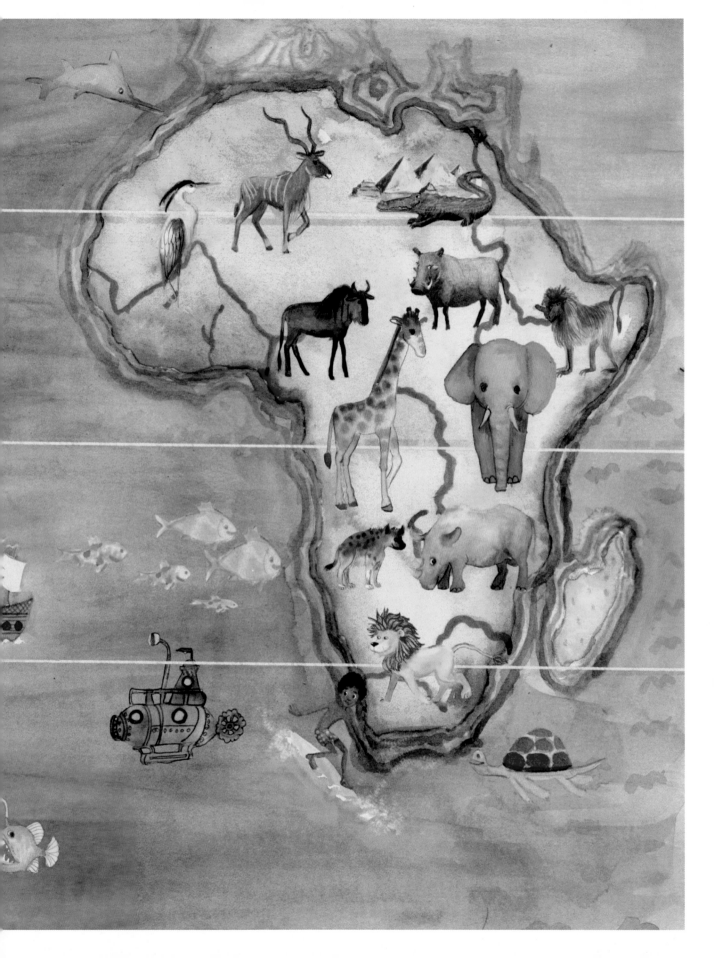

Fun Facts!!

Lion,
A lion's tongue is covered in small spikes called papillae. It has a variety of uses including cleaning dirt from its fur and assisting with their meals.

Hippo,
Hippos are semi-aquatic animals, they spend up to 16 hours of their day in water.

Hyena,
Hyenas create a yelping noise that resembles laughing, it is used as communication between each other.

Giraffe,
The neck of a giraffe can reach a length of 7 feet and weigh up to 600 pounds.

Kudu,
The horns of a kudu can reach up to 6 feet long.

Warthog,
Warthogs wallow in mud to reduce their body temperature and help avoid certain insects.

Fun Facts continued,

Crocodile,
Crocodiles receive dental assistance from Plover birds, they help clean the crocodile's teeth to prevent infection.

Elephant,
An elephant's hearing is so sensitive they can hear frequencies 20 times lower than humans.

Baboon,
Baboons along with many other animals enjoy consuming a native fruit called Marula. There are myths about the effects of a fermented version of this fruit on the local animals.

Heron,
There are over 70 species of Heron, the Black crowned night Heron has been known to make a loud barking sound when disturbed.

Coming soon.

Goodnight Australia

Goodnight North America

Goodnight Asia

Goodnight South America

Goodnight Europe

A Tale Of Two Rabbits: The Missing Heirloom.